Polio Boulevard

Also by Karen Chase

KAZIMIERZ SQUARE
(poems)

LAND OF STONE:
Breaking Silence Through Poetry

BEAR
(poems)

JAMALI-KAMALI:
A Tale of Passion in Mughal India

Polio Boulevard

A Memoir

KAREN CHASE

excelsior editions
State University of New York Press
Albany, New York

Back cover photo © 2014 Matthew Chase-Daniel

Published by State University of New York Press, Albany

Excelsior Editions is an imprint of State University of New York Press

For information, contact State University of New York Press, Albany, NY
www.sunypress.edu

Production by Jenn Bennett
Marketing by Fran Keneston

Library of Congress Cataloging-in-Publication Data

Chase, Karen.
  Polio boulevard : a memoir / Karen Chase.
    pages cm. — (Excelsior editions.)
  ISBN 978-1-4384-5282-1 (pbk. : alk. paper)
  1. Chase, Karen Block—Health. 2. Poliomyelitis—Patients—New York (State)—New York—Biography. 3. New York (N.Y.)—Biography. I. Title.

RC180.C48 2014
616.8'35—dc23   2013039419

10 9 8 7 6 5 4 3 2 1

For Richard Block, Maggi Walker, and Patsy Ostroy,
and to the memory of my parents,
Lil and Zenas Block

Contents

BEDS

Everything leads me back to my polio days now. Last week I drove to a used bookstore on back roads to pick up a biography of Jonas Salk. I noticed a junky antique store, pulled over, puttered through. An old piece of furniture was chained to the store's side porch—a hospital bed from upstate, where there had been a tuberculosis sanatorium long ago. It was oak and painted a darkish green. The works that made it go up and down were cast iron, and they were painted green too. The springs were spiraling. I fell in love with the bed and bought it.

The next morning, Memorial Day, I woke at six to meet the fellow who delivered the bed in his pickup. He unloaded it, I gave him a check, he left. I dragged the hose out, filled a pail with soapy water, scrubbed the thing down, and let it dry in the rising sun. The foam mattress in the basement just fit. I put a rose-colored sheet on it and dragged the bed under the maple tree. The day was just beginning.

Lying on this not-just-any bed brings me back to how full of motion the world was as I watched it from my polio bed. Everything but me seemed to be moving. I was immobilized in New York, high up on a hospital ward overlooking the East River. I was horizontal, covered in plaster, couldn't get out of bed, couldn't sit, couldn't walk. I was flat. I had a view of the river, and what I did was watch.

I watched boats pass from morning to night. I watched smoke billowing out of huge smokestacks, cars heading south on the FDR Drive, cars heading north, a helicopter flying across the sky, a jet carving a diagonal line across the blue as it took off from LaGuardia, boats moving, water moving. I watched the river's current.

One day I was looking out the window when a submarine surfaced right in front of the hospital. It was sunny, I'm sure of it, and slowly the sub rose from the water. A bunch of uniformed sailors appeared on deck. Airy and light, it was the sight of victory.

From my bed, I would look out the window across the river to Queens as morning came. It would be barely dark. A light bulb would go on in a window and cast a sweet orange gleam—artificial, antiquated. I'd wonder about the person who turned the light on— why were they getting up so early, where were they going? I always had them going. They'd be going and I'd be watching.

It's taken me decades to walk over to my desk, sit down once and for all, and write about what happened when I was a ten-year-old girl with polio.

Here I go. It's November. It's 1953. My family is living in the well-to-do village of Larchmont, New York, on Long Island Sound. I'm in fifth grade.

For lunch Mom makes me a peanut butter and jelly sandwich cut in the shape of a house. When I'm done, instead of heading back to school, I go lie down on the bed in the TV room.

I'm resting, which I never do. I don't even feel like watching TV. Look. There's one leg up in the air. My leg, I keep looking at it, I like looking at it. Maybe it hurts. Maybe it feels rusty or something. I'll say it hurts, and maybe I can stay home this afternoon. I don't want to give that book report.

My knees are skinned. When I was little, I used to sneak down near the beach with Jimmy Keenan. We liked to climb up on the roof of an old brick garage, jump off onto the ground. Sometimes my knees got scraped, and my legs got bruised.

I like my legs. I don't know why. They're just legs, but *just legs* is great. I like the bones of them, how they join. Some people talk about legs that are particularly long. My mother's are particularly bony. Mine aren't particularly anything.

I just swallowed, I *noticed* I swallowed. Just did it again. The back of my throat feels small and getting smaller.

I looked at the clock a few minutes ago. Now I look at it again, but the minute hand has hardly moved. I can hear my baby sister fooling around outside.

I better get up, I've got to start back to school. Today is going so slowly. I wait for minutes to pass. Look at the clock. Ow ow ow—my leg does kind of hurt. But after school, Patsy and I are going to bike to Flint Park.

It's the next day. The doctor comes into my room. He helps me sit on the edge of my bed. He opens his black bag, takes out a rubber mallet. Tap. He taps my knee. My leg does not move.

In the hospital, all I wanted to do was go home. People said, "Do this, do that," and I had to do it.

"Time for hot packs," a nurse would say.

"No. I want to go *home*."

I'd sleep all the time, wake up not knowing what day it was, not knowing if days or hours had passed.

Everyone was talking. Talking in the hall, nurses talking, doctors talking, visitors. I hated that sound.

Footsteps in the hall—are my parents here? I'm burning, my body's hurting, I'm nothing, a blank buzz of sleep.

"Strawberry milkshake," I said to my father. When he brought it, I couldn't stand the smell. The pink made me sick.

One day I asked for a book. The nurse said, "Wait a minute." She came back with an Archie and Veronica comic. When I tried to hold it, it dropped.

"Darling," my mother wrote to me in the hospital three months after I got sick.

I just heard the GOOD NEWS—you are standing and getting into the wheel chair alone.

I know this made you happy as it did me. Honey, this is another important hurdle you've jumped. I have a hunch (unofficial) you are on the homeward stretch.

Try very hard honey.

Well so long. I'll see you Sunday—I can't wait either.

Your Ma

THE BUS BACK

It's winter, it's night, I daydream. Town after town flies by. The bus drops me off on the corner where I grew up. Clothed in a long wool military coat, I speed along back streets in the snow, slipping on patches of ice, heading toward Long Island Sound.

There's the Leary's old house—thirteen kids. They drank a ton of milk, our milkman reported. I lag in front of this dark house, that dark house. "I'll never make it to the Sound." *Just move along on this ride toward the past.*

A bundled-up man with a Great Dane approaches. Like a soldier, I extend my hand. "Nice dog!" If my timing is off, my hand could be gone. Mechanically, I twist my head around. Will I ever be able to get back out of here? *There's nothing to fear.*

The water is getting closer, though; I smell that low-tide stench I smelled when I was a little girl. The mailbox in front of our old house no longer says The Blocks. I'm traversing the street above what history books say was the Underground Railroad. History books say history is big—wars, plagues. History is small, I say.

When I finally reach the Sound, I stand on the rocks and watch the water. Eventually, I get hungry and head back to town. I finish a tuna sub on wheat at Subway, which I paid for with dimes. I trundle across the street in the high wind and make my way to the Post Road Junk Store. On a shelf, I notice a matchbook collection in a scrapbook. There's one advertising War Bonds, one for Waldorf Cafeterias, one for RCA Victor. There's one for *Sunset Boulevard*, for *Stalag 17*, for the New York New Haven and Hartford, one for Playland at the Beach, for Orange Crush, for Mighty Mouse, for Macks Drugs, Hotel Piccadilly, Hotel Roosevelt. There's

JOIN THE MARCH OF DIMES
HELP
Fight Infantile Paralysis
NOW
SEND YOUR DIMES TO YOUR PRESIDENT

Scraps of bright color and word, page after page of actual matchbooks, concrete little squares of history. History looms small and large all at once. Strike a match for history.

Where were you when Malcolm X was shot? Where were you months later when the power went out in New York? The cityscape was lit in uncanny dark. My second son had just been born. 1965.

Where you were when you heard that the Twin Towers had collapsed is the spot where your history and the world's meshed. Your life widened out, wove into the public web. Some of you weren't even born yet, but your time will come.

History is confusing. I have come to see that history is like a braid, that you and I and everyone else interweave. History is big, history is small. History happened to you and to everyone too.

My mother and I are together, traveling fast in an ambulance. Her hazel eyes are open wide, her face tight. Feverish, I am looking out the window. A breeze moves the highest limbs of a maple. A bird parts the air.

I'm burning up. When we zoom past school, I look at the whizzing brick wall and think *book report,* and then I don't think anything.

The ambulance pulls up to a hospital. Men slide me fast out the back of it. My father, who has followed the ambulance in our car, is standing with my mother. They're like large guards, unmoving. The men slide me around on the ambulance stretcher. My body is frozen. The earth, earthquake-like, is shaking.

"Karen," my father tells me later, "your mother's hair turned white that year."

Soon, hot and tiny, I'm swimming in a sea. There is water and me, and me swimming hard as I can in a blackening bigness. My solid parents are an enlarging wooden raft.

I am attached to something crazy, some crazy transportation. The ambulance stretcher? No, the rush of the iron lung, which helps me breathe. The iron lung is an ivory enameled metal tube with chrome portholes and rests steady on the wooden ward floor. All my limbs are concealed. My head, separated from the rest of me on a slanted headrest, sticks out. I cannot move my head or anything at all.

The iron lung is my magic boat, a boat for one. A rhythm boat, in out, in out, in out. The portholes suggest foreign places. My body is inside the iron lung, but my mind is outside. I'm traveling.

I love traveling, both mentally and actually. In the summer of 1970, with extra gas cans strapped to the roof of a rented Land Rover, my husband and I and our two small sons headed for Askja, a live volcano in the interior of Iceland.

There we stayed in a cabin built for Neil Armstrong while he was training for the first human voyage to the moon. NASA had chosen the site because it was the place on earth that most resembled the moon.

I have a slide of the caldera. My husband has climbed the side of a huge crater to take the picture. You can see the inverted cone of another crater filled with a milk-white sulfurous lake. The large navy blue lake to the left is from another, earlier eruption. The mountain range in the distance—see it?—rocky and snow-covered, is on the edge of an area of ancient eruptions.

If you look in the lower left-hand corner, in that lonesome, spacious scene, there's a deep blue mountainous shape. It's my husband's dungaree-covered knee. He's leaning back to take the picture, and his knee is in the way. Little white dots on the lava-covered field in the far distance are not imperfections in the slide. Those dots are my two sons and me. At Askja, I loved the space.

I'm claustrophobic, paralyzed in the iron lung. Nurses bring me loads of mail. An envelope of St. Christopher medals and crucifixes comes from kids at the church near our house, but I'm too sick to care. A nurse slips a cold medal into my hand, but I can't grip it. It drops to the floor. I can't turn my head to see, but I hear the sound. *Tink.*

The nurse is reading me a letter from my best friend, Patsy. It includes our favorite silly rhyme.

> Hi lo inny minny kie kie
> unk kie chow chow
> o pee wow wow
> yup taminika zumpt ta platy umpt.

"Try to say this in one breath," Patsy writes. I can't. I have no breath.

I have nothing called day, nothing called night. I'm in space. No anything o'clock. The crying I hear, is it me? No, couldn't be. I'm too weak to make noise.

Looking for locomotion, I watch dots on the ceiling tiles. A camel walks from one corner straight across the ceiling to the other. Chickens peck the dots—chicken feed—their heads jerking up and down. A dotted horse runs fast and far over the dotted field. My iron capsule nearly budges from this unreal motion. I melt down inside the lung and am nauseated.

No windows in this hot universe, but curtains white and wild, the ceiling my barnyard, or my desert with tents afloat, red flags waving for help. No, the flags are white. All color has drained out. Humped camels parade, wear a path across the dotted albino moon.

I imagine walking so hard that my body rises from the capsule. Dizzied, I'm afloat.

The iron lung is my flying boat. I'm inside and outside it. Inside and outside meld like tropical space. My body looks out the portholes. I hear the *hoo hoo* of foghorns. Lying there paralyzed and out of breath, I'm traveling.

Hoo hoo—I hear it. When I was growing up in our house on the Sound long before I was sick, I'd lie awake and listen to the foghorn, wonder about boats passing.

A few years after the iron lung time, I was back home from a different hospital, again unable to move, this time encased in a full-length body cast. Early in the mornings, I'd hear that haunting *hoo hoo* warn boats away from the rocks—boats coming from somewhere and going somewhere. It didn't dawn on me that I would ever go anywhere. I was so busy picturing boats and where they were headed that I didn't care.

When I was put in the cast, I was like a road paved with cement. Doctors gave me a huge hard plaster skin. Years later an old friend said I had looked like a monster, the man in the moon. She wanted to get out of my room fast. She was scared.

I was alien, rocketing away from myself.

I'm traveling for real again, in Iceland again. My husband, sons, and I are waiting for Great Geysir to blow. There's a pungent smell, like medicine or rotten eggs. We've traveled all day on rough roads to reach this place, after which all geysers are named. Colors are all around—yellows, pinks, and greens layered on the hills. It's all sulfur, and that's what stinks.

Thar she blows! The earth takes a breath, spits water from its lungs. The sight is mesmerizing. Hot wet steam spews high into the air. They say "Thar she blows" when a whale is sighted, or "*Elle souffle*" (she breathes) if they're French. I say the earth's mouth is a blowhole.

Thermal springs abound in this naked land. Hothouses harbor tomato crops, heated by underground steam. In one town, greenhouses line the streets. All over the land, houses get heat from the earth's generous vaporous steam. Reykjavik, the name of the capital, means "City of Steam."

The land is a body exposed, barely any bushes or trees. Moss covers the land so you see its shape. When heat builds up too much inside the earth's body, volcanoes erupt like disease.

The history of the natural world is in plain view. No forests or cities hide the story of Iceland's scar-covered body. Craters, calderas, milky white lakes. Lava all over, old and new. Mud pools bubble, steam holes spew, large mouths in the ground.

When the earth gets sick, faults widen and it breaks apart. The earth's crust shifts. Anytime, its glassy rind can crack. Boom. Natural disaster—a plague arrives.

I return from Iceland and begin to write all the time, a first in my life. The exposed, unclothed landscape spurred me to mentally undress. Before then, I painted. Now it was time for words.

Polio did not cast a shadow on my life. I appeared unscathed. While I was sick, my parents urged me to talk to a psychiatrist to face my fears. Would I learn to walk again? Would I be crippled? In fact, these fears belonged to other people, not to me. My way was not to dwell on difficulty, but to move forward. I didn't see a psychiatrist. Denial allowed me to hold on to my optimism. Now, years later, I am keen to explore the country of illness.

INTRUDERS

I'm the mother of young sons. We have recently moved from a city apartment to a house on a lake in a town. I love being in the country. Royal blue tiles finally cover our kitchen floor, the grout a light terra cotta. The glass-doored cupboards are done, the workmen are gone. Our house is quiet and glistens. I go to the cellar for I don't know what. At the foot of the stairs lies a large dead rat.

Another move to another house on a lake, my children almost grown. On a beautiful day, my husband and I leave for work. As we walk through the mudroom, we can hear busy sounds in the ceiling.

"Probably mice," says Abilene Pest Control. I leave the house, and it starts to rain. When I get home, the noise is worse. I pick up a boot from the floor, toss it to the ceiling, hoping to stop the sound.

Hundreds of yellowjackets fly out. The boot has broken through the sheetrock. Wasps have thinned the ceiling. I move like lightning, close the door, contain the swarm, drive fast to the hardware store.

I buy a night bomb to release when the wasps return to their hive. Next day, they are all dead.

For decades, polio terrified America, killing and crippling at random. It lurked anywhere, came on as easily as a cold. Any fever, any stiff neck or sore throat caused hysteria.

A medical book from the 1940s: "The most perfectly housed and cared for child may acquire the disease, while the most neglected, unwholesomely housed child may escape it."

Each summer morning, one friend's mother arrived at her bedside to ask, "Do you have a stiff neck?" Another friend's frantic mother wouldn't let her play out back with ants.

A letter from my fifth-grade teacher arrived a week after I was struck.

We are all so sorry you are sick. We miss you so much. Quite a few children were absent last week, so we didn't do much work. Everyone seemed to have a sore throat. The speaker for Book Week lost us halfway through his speech. It was bedlam.

EARTHQUAKE

"No speaka Eeenglesh," was my mother's response when I used to ask her about it. She refused to discuss it. The only evidence of the earthquake in my parent's house was the cardboard carton in the cellar, shoved too close to the hot water heater. Broken dishes were in it, blue and white willow ware.

When I asked my father about the dishes, he gave a lengthy explanation that began with the geological makeup of our town—never got to the dish part.

The bedrock of our town was steady. There were green hills, green fields, and dark green woods, and there was the Sound. The tide went in and out. The danger of earthquakes was nil—no faults here.

The day of the earthquake, my mother, looking for comfort, kept running back and forth from her mother's house to ours. The hill slowly tilted. Its angle turned steep. Suddenly the air thickened. Smoke filled the whole sky. Breathing took concentration. Each inhalation hurt her lungs more.

A mudslide began, so that my mother, going up the incline, kept slipping down. There was no such thing as traction. Traction was over.

The sky was no longer a clear blue plate. Now it settled on her head. Ash settled upon her hair, turned it white.

On the anniversary of the earthquake each year, my mother nonchalantly waited for my father to go to work and for us kids to go to school. She locked the front and back doors and closed the shutters. She put on *The Pearl Fishers* loud, then went to her French cupboard, chose her favorite dish, and heaved it across the hard kitchen floor, made from quarry tile. She smashed the dish she loved to smithereens. Silently, with control, she swept up the shards and dumped them into the carton in the basement.

The day of the earthquake, my mother saw the trunks of the oldest standing trees severed as if with a cleaver. Their limbs turned rubbery and folded down like a closed umbrella.

Twenty years to the day after I was rushed to the hospital, I came upon my mother weeping in the living room.

When I was grown, I went back to our village to see the damage. Large buildings had been built, and a shopping mall had replaced some fields. At heart, though, it was the same. Where the ground had gone up in a gentle slope, it still went up. Where the earth had sloped down toward the Sound, it still did. Underneath the changes, it still was wide and flat where it once had been. The ample verandas on the oversized wooden houses that lined the broad avenue were still there.

"Verandas," my mother is saying to my father, and I don't know what she means. Next fall I will get sick, but now it's summer, and we are all okay, and we're driving in the Smokies—my parents, my brother, and me. My mother is about to have a baby, my sister, a few months later. Something beginning and something ending. But today it's still just the four of us, traveling by car.

My father slows down, pulls over to Starvin Marvin's, a restaurant and fish pond. My brother and I each get a pole and start to fish. When one bites, I ignite like a struck match and pull it in. My father takes my fish off the line and brings it into the restaurant to be cooked for our lunch!

"Sugar doll," a man there calls my mother. I want him to call me that too. The day is good and so is lunch.

When we pass a sign that says Tonite Church Supper Roast Pork, my godless Jewish parents make jokes. We're having a great trip, speeding along.

The year before I got sick, I loved with no reserve. I loved going crabbing with my father in the shallow, muddy inlet of Long Island Sound, loved how we wouldn't stop until we got a full pail, then how he'd boil them up for dinner. My mother planted a bed of high painted zinnias around our raised slate terrace. Those reds and oranges and pinks looked like they came straight from her paint tubes. The summer passed, and Maggi was born in the fall.

I was excited before that summer, and I was excited after. Loved painting, loved color, loved to swim, loved the water, the air, loved to breathe, loved jumping, jump rope, hopping, hopscotch, loved that picture window in my brother's bedroom from which you could see the water.

I loved what grew: buttercups, peaches, swamp grass. I loved Patsy, my next-door neighbor and best friend. I loved watching her German father work his dark, crumbly soil. Leo grew high red cannas, a semicircle patch of them near their screened-in porch. That chilly, darkish porch with a stone floor and varnished rattan furniture that he bought while on business in the Far East. He imported pocketbooks. The Far East, what's that? I wondered. My father was American, younger, full of experiments, game for anything. He'd sit on the lawn at war with the crabgrass, a trowel in his grubby hand to get it by the roots. My dad planted a white peach tree, planted a grape arbor, made a vat of crabapple jelly from our tree. He was a food chemist and worked for the Doughnut Corporation of America.

Sometimes that summer I found myself biking down the broad main avenue of our town, passing those houses with verandas on my way to the beach. Then fall arrived.

THIS IS MY FATHER TALKING

ZENAS BLOCK: Test it.

KAREN CHASE: No, I can tell it's recording.

ZB: I have to sit in that chair. This is too low for me.

KC: Okay . . . Dad, do you want, like, a chair to put your feet up?

ZB: No.

KC: That's not more comfortable?

ZB: No, I'm all right. Don't worry.

KC: So, I don't know. I made a whole list of questions somewhere, but I don't know what to ask. Where can we start? I've been, um, I . . .

ZB: Yeah. Well, one way, you know, to start talking about this is the, um, the earliest image I have. It was dark, and the doctor coming and examining you—

KC: Yeah.

ZB: —and saying, "It's polio."

An ambulance coming to take you to Grasslands . . . uh, and I remember what was going through my mind and Mother's mind, the first thing was—will you live? That was the first thing, would you live?

I sort of remember the iron lung, which you think you never were in, but I think you were in for a short while—

KC: No, Dad. I know I was.

ZB: The day we took you to the hospital. That was horrifying. An ambulance came. It was an overcast, cold November day . . . and you and Mom got into the ambulance, and I followed. We stayed there very, very late—kept going back until . . . until your life was no longer in danger. I remember looking at other kids. There was one—grotesquely tiny, with bones that didn't grow. She was cheerful—she looked like an elf or dwarf.

The whole Grasslands thing was very, very foggy in my mind, you know. I can't remember it clearly . . . and I guess the reason is, I was blocking it out, trying to block it out.

The hazard of your getting sick, destroying the family, destroying my ability to make a living, just dragging us down. I decided I was just not going—I was not, you know. *Just keep functioning somehow, just shut everything out.* Then we knew you were going to live. We knew what you couldn't do. But the big question was, the overwhelming question was—were you going to be a hunchback?

That is very vivid. All the trips to Dr. Cobb, the discussions. The whole long process began of deciding when and if to do the surgery, the spinal fusion.

To me, that was the most critical event in the history of the thing. The decision to do it—the doubt as to when to do it, and whether it was too early to do it, and what the consequences would be.

Sitting over X-rays with Dr. Cobb, I remember that, and his drawing lines, showing the curvature of your spine. His saying, "It's up to you to decide." Against operating was that if your spine kept growing it would split the fusion. And it would have to be done all over again. If we delayed, there was the chance of serious deformation. That was it. To me, that was nightmarish. My fear of having made a decision that would make you go back into a cast for x more years, a repeat operation, or letting you turn into a hunchback. It was unbelievable. Because I had to make the decision. Mother and I.

I cross-examined Dr. Cobb.

"Well, what is the evidence you look for, to determine whether or not bone growth has stopped?"

"Well, we look at the wrist bones."

"What do you see in the wrist bones?"

I was just cross-examining him left and right.

"What do you think the probabilities are? How certain are you?"

Of course, there was nobody else—nobody else who could help. It was a nightmare—those x-rays of your curved spine with the lines going through them and the angle of measurement every time we went to the doctor. Seeing the angle gradually increasing. I wanted to, uh, I wanted to keep you at home. And we kept you at home. We had a hospital bed; we had nurses come.

It was sort of a division. Mother was intimately familiar with everything going on. I was pushing it away. If I didn't, we'd go under, I felt. Well, she was . . . she was unbelievable, totally dedicated. I think it was horrible for her. It was horrible, but she also just sort of—it was what it was. *You had to do what you had to do and you just did it.*

I think essentially it was, although because of her, in a real sense, slavery to the situation, I mean, she was absolutely totally—you know, I would go off to work, and she would be . . . giving you bedpans. I mean, she must have felt differently, although—and, you know, I don't recall her ever breaking down or crying, other than just at the time you got sick.

People were amazed at you in the cast—everybody came to see you. You were hauled all over the place— upstairs, downstairs, outside, everywhere. It weighed over two hundred pounds. We dragged you all over the house. I'd carry you up and down the steps.

When you ask me what it was like when I first saw you in the cast, I'm at a total loss as to what you mean. What do you mean, what was it like? What it was like was, you were in a cast, surrounded by plaster, you were immobile, you had to be moved around. That's what it was like. I don't know what else to say about that.

ZB: You know, before you got sick you were like an otter.

KC: Like a what?

ZB: An otter.

KC: What do you mean?

ZB: You know what an otter is, don't you?

KC: Yeah, but I don't know what you mean.

ZB: You swam. You loved being in water, and it's in the water that you reminded me of an otter. You'd have to see an otter to see how it swims on its back and is playful in the water. Well, it's the most flexible, acrobatic water animal that you ever saw, you know, and you were just so graceful and so swift, you know, and I kept thinking about that, and . . . some of that has carried through, even with, after the polio, but before the polio it was, I mean, you were such a physically competent child, it was unbelievable.

You were a pain in the ass, demanding, interrupting— but, you know, you were an exciting child, an adorable little girl, because you tried all kinds of things. You were brave, I admired you, and then, uh, when you got sick . . . my feeling about you just completely—you know, then it was a question of protecting you and seeing that you got through it all. I wanted you to live and be able to move.

KC: Dad, do you remember—it must have been soon after the war, and I used to look out the window and wait for the lights of your car to come home from work. I think the car was beige, anyway, and I think I got to go with you, alone, to go pick it up when it was new.

ZB: I'm trying to remember when I had the Chevy convertible, which one it was. Did I have a Chevy convertible? No, my first car was not a Chevy convertible.

KC: What was it?

ZB: It was a Chevrolet coupe.

KC: What color?

ZB: Well, after the accident, it was red. I smashed it up. I was driving in upstate New York in the middle of the war period. I had gone down to Manhattan to buy a fan, a big industrial fan that we were installing in our onion drying plant—

I was driving through the snow up to Middletown, thought the road went straight ahead and at the last minute realized it turned, and I turned right into a head-on collision. No one was hurt.

During World War II, I worked all the time, worked seven days a week, making instant coffee and other rations for the army. That stopped in '45.

It all boiled down to what happened to your spine. You had recovered a good deal of mobility; you had a couple problems with your hands, which you still have—

KC: What? What about my hands?

ZB: Oh, this muscle was . . . didn't exist. Do that. (He demonstrates.) Try to flex that muscle. There isn't one.

KC: What are you doing that I'm not doing?

ZB: Just pressing this and flexing this muscle. You don't have one.

DREAMBOAT

Suddenly I see him in a black bathrobe. He's walking to the podium. He's gripping the podium with his strong hands. He has spent years perfecting the illusion of walking. No, it's not my father, it's somebody else! Now he's leaning against the podium. *Leaning*, that's the main thing.

FDR's black robe billows out. His strong-boned face looks polished, like a stone memorial.

A thread of balance holds him up. When the wind blows, maybe he'll fall. Exposed are heavy black steel braces encasing his withered legs. He has just returned from Marrakesh. There he was carried up a mountain to see the sun set. Next thing, daylight.

I'm anybody in the audience, watching newsreels. A man in black trousers and black hat is addressing Congress now. His shiny braces are outside his pants. He no longer conceals them. Now, I swear, he's wearing gold lamé shoes! I can't breathe.

I wake up, go pee, can't fall back to sleep, and start to count. Soon after a thousand, I switch to sound—*va va voom. Va va voom,* I repeat, but remain alert. Then *va voom* works, and finally I sleep.

Another newsreel. The man is wheeling around a racetrack on a maroon tufted armchair. The gong goes off. His chair speeds around the course. He has a rust-colored leg on his lap and a blue enameled axe. The wind swirling in the distance has a stormy smell.

Pretzels litter the track. One birch bends down at the edge of the screen, heavy with spring snow. Pretzels jerk around like jumping beans, lift up the armchair. Stars mix together in the purple sky and then flop in a heap to the ground.

In the casbah, FDR is relaxing, drinking vodka with Winston Churchill late at night. What's a casbah? Smoking a cigar, he puffs smoke rings into the air, watches them alight. "There's nothing to fear," he says as wind blows and buries the casbah in sand.

A silky sash around his steel waist holds closed his coral wool coat, like one my grandmother made for me when I was little and could run really fast. His feet are clad in bandaged white boots. The newsreel stops.

The sky lightens, the air is washed—it's never been so full of promise, so clear, so new, as if there had never been a war.

Out in the bristling air, Roosevelt and I are perambulating together, citizens of this great land.

DATES

Franklin Delano Roosevelt, a young politician, noticed a forest fire while sailing in the Bay of Fundy one morning in August 1921. He was not yet the governor of New York, not yet the president of the United States of America. He and his children rushed ashore and broke off pine branches to fight the flames. By the end of the afternoon, exhausted, they returned to Campobello, their summer home. They jogged across the island and swam in a freshwater lagoon. Then, for "refreshment," FDR went for a quick dip in the freezing bay.

He was "too tired to dress" by the time he got home and sat in his wet bathing suit, reading mail. "I didn't feel the usual reaction, the glow I'd expected," he said later. Chilled, he walked up the stairs without supper.

The next morning, "when I swung out of bed, my left leg lagged, but I managed to move about to shave. I tried to persuade myself that the trouble with my leg was muscular . . . But presently it refused to work, and then the other."

Roosevelt never walked again.

History is embarrassing. It's embarrassing to be part of history. My life is small, history is big, best to stay small. You can hold the matchbooks of history in your hand.

My life is small, your life is small, my town is small and always was. If you don't make the connections, you can stay small, but all and all, history is big. And so are you and so am I because we're people and we're alive.

It's embarrassing to write about yourself because of what my mother said. Best to be a lady, private and dignified. But she did give me a great fountain pen with a fat point. Was it her way of urging me to be bold?

For Roosevelt, anything less than history was embarrassing. History was him, and he would make it, and what a job he would do. He was a patrician, and I'm from peasant Ashkenazi stock. He was a man and I was a girl.

I'm five, and it's April. First thing each day, we sit on the wooden floor in a semicircle around our teacher. She sits on a small wooden chair. She holds a pencil and a light blue soft-covered notebook in which she takes attendance. She says a name. If it's yours and you're there, you say, "Present."

When she gets to the F's, she starts, in slow motion, to erase. Now she's blowing the rubber eraser crumbs off the page. She's saying, "Cindy Faulkner died in a car accident." The car caught fire.

Yesterday Cindy sat with us on the floor. She was wearing a bright yellow dress with smocking, I'm sure.

History, small history, bigger than any war.

"It is dark all over the world," the great TV commentator Edward R. Murrow is saying. It is March 4, 1933. "Japan is already in Manchuria. The League of Nations is dying in Geneva. In Germany the Reichstag fire is history. So is the Weimar Republic. In rich fertile America fear and uncertainty lay heavy upon the land.

"'Our greatest primary task is to put people to work.' Franklin D. Roosevelt stands beside Chief Justice Hughes on the steps of the Capitol on this raw afternoon and a nation with fifteen million unemployed, listen."

Roosevelt is not standing; he is leaning. Now he's talking.

"So first of all, let me assert my firm belief that the only thing we have to fear is fear itself—nameless, unreasoning, unjustified terror which paralyzes needed efforts to convert retreat into advance."

He was paralyzed, I was paralyzed, and on May 26, 1985, my mother died of cancer. There's so much illness in the world.

I went to Provincetown the next July. "In May, my mother died," I wrote.

Then I tried: "Years ago after my mother had died, I went to Cape Cod and rode through the dunes on my bike."

Then: "In the midst of summer, just over two months since her mother died, she's at the Cape not doing anything."

Then: "A month after Hazel's mother died, she went to the ocean and watched the tide come in for weeks on end."

Then: "After your mother died, you went to the Maine coast for awhile. You helped me pick periwinkles for money. See—see in that photo—that pail you're holding is full of periwinkles. You're too young to remember."

History is hard to grasp, no matter how hard you try.

History happened to you, not just you but everyone. If you're younger, it was 9/11. If you're a bit older, it was the *Challenger*. If you're my age, it was Jack Ruby killing Lee Harvey Oswald right on TV.

Roosevelt's death happened to your mother, not just your mother but everyone's mother.

The Second World War happened to your parents, not just your parents but everyone's parents. Or your grandparents or your great-grandparents. The Second World War happened to you too, because history lasts.

Because history lasts, it happened to you too. John Lennon died, and Indira Gandhi and Napoleon, and that girl in my kindergarten class.

Polio scared everyone. Parents, grandparents, cousins, uncles, aunts—families were terrified of polio. Schools were, camps were; pick any group, and they were terrified. FDR feared for his children while sailing the Bay of Fundy that summer morning.

Nieces got polio, nephews got it, someone's cousin got it, a family friend, a kid on your block, a kid in your class, one you liked, one you didn't like, and there they were, paralyzed. Braces, crutches, wheelchairs, or dead.

The fear of polio that swept across the country was not new. Numerous epidemics broke out in the twentieth century. The summer of 1916 saw one of the worst. A newspaper reported, "Panic froze the East, particularly New York City where 2,000 died and another 7,000 were attacked, three-fourths of them children under five. Thousands tried to leave—police at highways and railroad stations halted them. Few hospitals would take polio cases. Police had to break into apartments to take dead children from their mothers."

Blue boxes of doughnuts arrived each Saturday morning by parcel post at our house in Larchmont, before I got sick. My father would line the boxes up on the mottled maroon linoleum counter. He'd chew a piece from the first box thoughtfully, furrow his brow, make notes on a long yellow pad, spit his mouthful out. On to the next. That was his job.

My mother's feet were bony, the linoleum was rubbery, her nearly black hair was kinky. I was living a little girl's life near New York.

We lived on California Road. My grandfather visited a place called California, brought me back an embroidered jacket that said "Mexico." The world was big.

In her youth, my mother had been expelled from the University of Maryland. She got herself into New York University, where she became the head of the Communist Party. At night, she'd go alone to the docks in Brooklyn, deliver secret messages to unknown people about unknown things. She had no idea what she was delivering.

Much later, when her father died, she said, "I was the apple of his eye." She got quiet. She began to paint abstract canvases and read biographies in bed in the afternoons. As I got older, she said, "Get a teaching degree for insurance." Huh?

She'd take me across the Harlem River Bridge on the train to New York for painting classes, even before she painted herself. I was four years old and splashing colors onto huge paper in a museum basement a few years after the war.

While my mother's history and my own were weaving together, my second husband, eleven years older than I, was sitting in a parlor in Passaic, New Jersey, listening to Edward R. Murrow warn about polio on the radio. His mother wouldn't let him go to the movies—no swimming, no crowds, no Bagel Beach. But he was unafraid.

History is braidlike. It turns out that little you (meaning me), and big history (meaning the news), and everyone else (meaning you and FDR), interweave.

HOSPITAL MAIL

My father called me Monkey, but I don't think I was the apple of his eye. Or maybe I was, I don't know.

Monkey,

I am sorry that I could not get up to see you today and I will surely be up next Wednesday (and also Sunday).

Darling, I'm not going to tell you that I miss you because I feel that we're all together every minute. I never stop thinking of you and I just know that you're going to be alright.

Mother told me all about the visit. Honey, I must tell you something which is very important.

If you can stop to think a moment, and forget about how you have felt some of the time, you will realize that you have been making steady, good progress in getting well. During the worst part of your illness, you had the courage to fight to get better. You have cooperated well with the doctors and Miss Mac. As you have gone into each ward, you've found people to have fun with—not everybody—but at least one in each place.

In other words, honey, you've met each situation as it came up and come through it O.K.

Now, when you are so much better, is the time that you have to fight the hardest. Now you feel well enough to be bored, to get lazy, and of course to go home.

If you let yourself get too bored, it stretches minutes into hours and hours into days. To make your stay in the hospital as bearable as possible, the main problem to overcome is how to pass time.

It's a funny thing, but that's the same problem most people have all their lives, and depending on how happily busy they are, that's how happily they spend their lives.

This is the first time in your life that you have to solve this problem. You are equipped better than most people to solve it. Reading, writing letters, embroidering, studying schoolwork, taking pictures, are all things you are able to do well. Why not do them? Each one is fun, and accomplishing things is the most fun of all.

Sweetie, try this stuff and see for yourself. Make out a schedule, roll up your sleeves and dive in.

Just remember that you are loved by lots of people and so awfully much by Mother, Rich and me. We never stop thinking about you and hoping for your quick recovery. So come on kid!

Love,
Dad

Hello Sweetheart,

I went out after lunch and bought these two pairs of pajamas for you. I do hope you like them.

Patsy sent you the dog magazine. She thought you might enjoy it, since you will be getting a puppy.

Darling girl, the nurse told me that you were eating better. I do hope this is really so.

Oh yes, they told me that I couldn't bring any chewing gum—that is why you are not receiving any today. But when you get home you can chew and chew.

I must stop now and hop into the car and take this up to you. We are all with you. Be a big brave girl.

Loads of love and kisses,

Your Mom

When I got sick, a few people sent the same get-well card. A cute bear wrapped in a blanket in a hospital bed, his eyes closed. The card says:

A DREAM BOOK to cheer you.
This "dream book" comes while you're in bed
And snoozin' quite a lot
To tell you what you'd better dream
And what you'd better not.

Inside the card, the wide-eyed bear sits up.

And then it brings a wish for you
That you'll get well so quick
That folks who didn't know it
Wouldn't dream
that you'd been sick.

Sickness was embarrassing. If you were sick, you were weak, and that was no good. FDR was skillful in this regard. The skill with which he fooled the public about his crippledness was matched by his passion to help others with polio and find a way to prevent it.

Send your dimes to your President. The Hollywood comedian Eddie Cantor thought those words should be broadcast over the radio. "We could call it the March of Dimes," he said. So FDR founded the March of Dimes, and radio appeals began. A few days later, truckloads of dimes kept pulling up to 1600 Pennsylvania Avenue. People's enthusiasm made them inventive. They sent dimes "baked into cakes, jammed into cans, imbedded in wax and glued into profiles of the President." The White House was drowning in dimes. "The government of the United States darned near stopped functioning," said the head of the mailroom. It was 1938.

In a state of delight, FDR sat around smoking cigarettes, watching mountains of coins accumulate. In the first appeal, 2,680,000 dimes were received.

Twelve years later, still no cure. It was summertime 1950, the threatening season. Our local paper reported how my little friends and I helped the national effort.

POLIO BENEFIT

Larchmont police today are in possession of an envelope containing $3.08, which was delivered to them yesterday afternoon by seven girls, all approximately seven years old, who asked that the money be turned over to the March of Dimes.

They revealed that the money represented the proceeds of a puppet show which they had conducted and that they wanted to give it to help less fortunate children.

Polio kept striking, as whimsical as a sneeze. From the *New York Times*, March 1953:

STATE RECOGNIZES SNEEZE
AS BASIS FOR JOB BENEFITS

The Court of Appeals ruled unanimously today that "receiving the discharge of a sneeze" was "as much of an accidental injury as receiving a blow from an involuntary or unintended movement of another's arm."

The board made the award to Miss Gladys Gardner, who said she had developed polio when a fellow nurse sneezed in her face while she was a student nurse.

In 1953, for about ten days after I took sick, I was on the critical list. It was unclear whether I would live. When the doctor told me I had a cold, I was so sick that I believed him. Then I was moved to the polio ward, Sunshine Cottage.

There I met a cheerful, undersized girl named Peggy who could not move a bit. Her bed looked like a crib. Jeff, who wore heavy steel braces, was quiet and sweet and was carried all over. There were others, but these were my friends. Dennis was my best friend. He had polio but now he could walk. You'd never know he was sick. He was thirteen and black. We read each other our mail, joked around every chance we got.

Mail is the best. Here's one from a camp friend:

Dear Karen,

Did you receive a letter from Quannicut Camp asking you to come to a camp gathering? I hear you said as bad as being sick is, camp was worse. Even though I am not sick, I think you are right.

Love and a million kisses from
Old Water Rat

This one is kind of funny, from the girl next door:

Every morning, noon and night I ask how you are. Everyone in school asks for you. I never knew so many people know you. I would like to give you the best present money can buy. Even if you fight with me, the best present I could get is that you are home.

Hot packs this afternoon. They take hot blankets out of a steaming machine, roll me up in them, wrap me tight until I cool down. Later Mac is coming to have me do leg lifts, arm lifts, and then I can't wait till Mom comes. I wonder what it's like at home. It's hard to even remember my baby sister Maggi. She must be so big now. I can't even think what she looks like. I get so homesick. I try not to cry, but sometimes I can't help it. It's almost lunchtime. There's snow outside.

I get a funny letter from my last year's teacher.

I have been teaching my kids about atomic energy. Some of the boys think they know so much about it, they are going to try to make an A bomb. You'll know they were successful if you hear a loud boom.

Boom. Dennis and Jeff and I are playing Monopoly. I have hotels on Marvin Gardens and Atlantic. I'm on a stretcher, Jeff's in his wheelchair, and Dennis sits on a regular chair. The radio is on.

Wait, wait—what's this?

Someone on the radio is saying that Dr. Somebody made a vaccine from monkeys—from rhesus monkeys. Dr. Jonas Salk minced up tissues from monkeys' kidneys and put them in test tubes with . . . what? People won't get polio anymore!

Dennis and I start to laugh. We get laughing so hard that a nurse comes over. Dennis keeps saying, "A little late." Jeff is really quiet. I say, "Monkey kidney, monkey kidney," and we start up again, laughing hysterically.

I hated history when I went back to school in ninth grade, hated my World History teacher, hated our World History book, its weight, its size. The paragraphs ran in double columns. I cheated on my history final and did not get caught.

My eleventh-grade boyfriend and I melted dimes—our personal March of Dimes. He made a ring mold just my size. From the liquid silver, he made a ring. Melting money is against the law, you know. We demolished dimes all one afternoon.

"Let's see—garlic, Parmesan, frozen ravioli, and peas." I'm buying groceries years later.

"$8.11," says the salesgirl. As I'm handing her a dime, I notice FDR's head. I hesitate, paw it. History's everywhere. She gives me a crooked look.

LOCOMOTION

The late, great actor Orson Welles is looking at the president of the United States. FDR is saying, "We are the two best actors in America." His braces painted black, he wears black pants cut long, black socks and shoes. Believing it is political suicide to look crippled, he employs camouflage and illusion.

"He developed this technique that *looked* like walking." I am riveted to a man in a wheelchair talking about Roosevelt on TV. "He would lean on one son's arm, putting all his weight on it. And then he would switch his weight from the son's arm onto a cane, which he carried in the other hand, so he could switch his weight from side to side and then progress.

"He instructed his sons—'You must not let people see that this takes effort or hurts.' They would chat and joke and laugh as they went along. They looked as though they were taking their time so they could smile at people, say hello to the crowd . . . It was show biz but it worked."[1]

---

1. Hugh Gallagher, *FDR's Splendid Deception: The Moving Story of Roosevelt's Massive Disability—and the Intense Efforts to Conceal It from the Public* (Vandamere Press, 1999).

He is carried to his place at the White House dinner table before guests arrive. The public never sees this. He detests it, but he is carried all over.

I'm stuck in bed, unable to pop right up and pee. Each unfree task of the day requires help. Someone has to open the shades. Someone has to get me a bedpan, close the curtain around my bed, crack the metal bar of the hospital bed down, fetch the pan when I'm done.

Someone has to bring me that kidney-shaped aluminum pan and a cup of water to brush my teeth. Someone has to take it away. Each task takes too long; every move is slowed down.

Two orderlies carry me to the solarium. The sun's moving. Suddenly the city's buildings are lit by the rising sun. Building after building lines up in shadow, in light. A place of worship, the world is washed from this height.

Sixteen now, I love to drive fast. I'm back at school, as if I had never left. I take my parents' two-toned Olds after a fight. I'm furious, on fire. Don't know why, don't care either. I speed to the water, park, go sit on the rocks.

I love to drive to the Long Island Sound and watch the water. The other day I made a painting of the rocks. I looked down at my tubes, got a coffee can and mixed water with blues. I put my hand in the can of blue water, then spritzed and splashed the canvas, splattered the rocks over and over, opening and closing my fist. Art is great. It's a great way to move.

FDR is driving fast through the Georgia backwoods. He loves to drive too. He designed his car with gizmos so he can locomote himself. He's driving a dirt road to Dowdell's Knob, up Pine Crest.

It's the high rock outcropping where he spends hours gazing at the changing light on the woods below. Sometimes he wears his braces outside his pants so he can get them off by himself up there, a great pleasure.

For him, any kind of locomotion will do. FDR loves boating too, so he buys himself an old beat-up houseboat. And he is the first president in history to fly in an airplane. He is reportedly so excited when he takes off that he acts like a sixteen-year-old. He writes:

> We flew north along the Coast. Then inland over the desert. Not flat at all & not as light as I had thought— more a brown yellow with lots of rocks and wind erosion.
>
> Then ahead a great chain of mountains—snowy top.
>
> I tried a few whiffs of oxygen—
>
> North of the Mts. we suddenly descended over the first oasis of Marrakech. We may go there if Casablanca is bombed.
>
> At last Casablanca & the ocean came in sight.

There FDR had secret war meetings with Churchill, whose daughter tells what happened a few days later:

> [My father and the president] set off together for a brief holiday across the Moroccan desert to Marrakech. My father said to the President, "You cannot come all this way and not see the sun set over the Atlas Mountains from Marrakech."

At the golden hour, the President had to be carried up to the tower. He was determined to see it from where my father said it should be seen. They sat at the top of the tower and they watched the sun set over the Atlas Mountains.[2]

What a sight it must have been—the desert, the sun slipping behind the mountains, the president of the United States of America being carried up to such a height.

2. Lady Mary Soames, *American Experience: FDR*, PBS. Air date: 1994.

BOWING DOWN

My friend Brother Adam was a honeybee researcher. When he died, his obituary reminded me of Roosevelt's ascent up the mountains: "In one example of his travels in search of native strains of bees, a fellow apiarist carried the 90-year-old Brother Adam on a bamboo chair strapped to his back up Africa's highest mountain, Mount Kilimanjaro. He couldn't make the climb himself." Nothing stops Brother Adam, I thought when he wrote me about the trip. He adored locomoting—a word he relished—by foot, by donkey, by boat, to remote corners of the earth. A Benedictine monk, he had lived in an English abbey from the time he was a young boy. After he took over the apiaries there, he traveled the globe in search of new strains of honeybees.

When he was ninety-four, he ended his scientific investigations because the monastery's new abbot ruled that the purpose of the abbey apiaries was honey production, not research. To the dismay of scientists worldwide, Brother Adam obediently bowed down, not to illness, but to the will of his superior.

You bow down when a force larger than you prevails. A virus requires you to bow down. You've left the land of ordinary days, ordinary nights. Bye-bye ordinary life. It doesn't matter what you want or think. Doctors say, "Do this. Do that." And you may as well submit. Hot with fever, you don't care what land you're in.

Brother Adam is sick in bed. "Tell me everything," he says. He's ninety-eight. The skin of his face is pleated, and he's wheezing. He paws the photo I've brought of my garden. "How's the rhubarb? Are the raspberries ripe? Has your husband put up his cordial yet?" Brother Adam's eyes are like wet grey stones on a beach. "Tell me everything. How was the train ride?" He purses his lips and waits for stories.

As I talk, his onionskin face moves. My words carry him to my garden as I describe the rhubarb stalks. He offers me butterscotch pudding from his food tray, wants to be sure I'm okay. He wants to hear about the book I'm writing. He wants news from the outside.

Then, with verve, he tells me where he was when he heard the announcement of the Salk vaccine. In a Moroccan backyard as he observed bees on a bush, a radio blared the discovery through an open door.

I tell him Jonas Salk's first words as a child were, "Dirt, dirt."

"Really?" he says, and gives a deep belly laugh. He loves this piece of news. He says, "Tell me more."

Brother Adam did not speak until he was past two, just made humming and buzzing noises. He loved to play with ants. He thinks that's when he started to notice how insects act.

Brother Adam dozes off, and I go to the hospital bathroom. A beautiful long-haired teen is there with a friend. Her body must be riddled with disease, but she can't tell yet. Her migration to the land of disease still seems far away. From the stall, I hear her say, "I can't die! I have a dress on layaway!"

She cannot accept that she will soon become just another wild beast, transformed by disease. A fawn chased by a toothy wolf. Meat. One in a million, a member of the animal kingdom. No will. No choice.

Whatever happens happens, and you submit. Fade out. Lie on your back. Wait to see what's next. Pray people know what they're doing to you. Are they doing right? You have no energy to find out. You may as well relax.

Some people will not submit to illness no matter what, as if they can escape, change their fate.

Franklin Roosevelt was often cheerful after he got polio, insistent that he would conquer his disease. He hated pity. But soon after he was carried up the mountains in Morocco to see the sun set, he blurted out to his pal Louis Howe, "Why has God forsaken me?"

No matter what the doctors said, FDR believed he would walk. For years, even until his death, he tried everything. Nothing worked. He amassed power in other ways, became president. Me, I submitted. Then I walked. Note: there is no cause and effect.

When I was sick, I watched Florence, the girl in the next hospital bed, refuse to submit. Her bed was her throne, the world her slave. For royalty, no hospital gowns. Her mother ran back and forth to the ward with freshly laundered clothes. If her mother brought the wrong shirt, Florence sent her home. Everything must be exact. People were summoned, dismissed.

Hospital food—ugh! Her trays came and went, untouched. She had her father bring the exact right lasagna and the exact right soup. She sent her sister out for the exact right cookie.

Her father ran to a deli for chicken salad. "Ugh, disgusting!" she said when she opened the package. "Throw it out! No, wait, I'll have a bit of bread."

The ward watched.

WATER IS COMPLICATED

Outside it's stormy from hell, gulls and bigger birds buffeted about, the waves keeping on, clouds flying by fast, and the wind keeps blowing open the window. I can't get it to stay shut. My room hangs over the harbor. The tide's high. Gulls screech.

Look at this picture, would you? It's Brother Adam, who will die in a few days. It's the last time he was outside. Look how he's staring, daring the camera to tell the truth.

The day the picture was taken, I wore a dress to visit him, a piece of thrift-shop finery, dropped waist, from the twenties. When I walked in, he said, "Your dress reminds me of Key West! I love to think of Key West!" He was so weak, it was hard for him to move his mouth, but his mind was traveling south. A long pause, then, "Do you think it would be crazy for me to go outside?"

It was morning, gorgeous, Indian summer. We got him into a wheelchair, wheeled him out. The ground was bumpy.

"Keep me moving," he mumbled.

Time slowed. We bumped him along across the lawn.

"How is it?" I asked quietly.

"Magic."

"Water," he says. "There's something complicated about water." Nothing can slake his thirst.

He asks for lemon sherbet to wet his parched gullet. "See how demanding I've become," he adds. It's almost funny, I almost laugh. Soon his speech begins to slur, then, "I want to run, run into the garden." He slips into sleep. The last words I hear: "I can't breathe." The day before: "Can't make noise." I lean over his bed, open the window to let air in.

Next day, sounds from his lungs filling with fluid begin.

I sit here watching the tide, watching the waves, reading Hart Crane, playing solitaire, then doing it again.

The evening Brother Adam died, the nurse said, "This could go on all night. Why don't you go home?" He was making horrendous sounds. The nurse did not want me to see.

When he said, "Tell me everything," he meant everything. He counted on me. He died at 8:33. The doctor came soon after and wrote out the death certificate, put down time of death, the time right then, but that's not when he died.

The tide is up to the dock. The lighthouse in the fog is far away. Copies of *The Inferno* are by my side, all three editions, plus the maroon leather one my parents gave me. I want them nearby, not to read.

Solitaire again.

Coffee again.

You have them, you lose them—*in out*—like tide, like breathing.

Waves again. I've seen something I never want to see again.

To feel better, I cooked myself a two-pound lobster, baked a potato, and kept playing solitaire.

Someone should paint the sky with the tide dead out—oranges, greens, lavenders, greys. All mud—light and color reflected on wet mud. My mother was a painter, did I tell you that? When I woke about half an hour ago, the wharf was a black silhouette.

Brother Adam drowned at the end as water filled his lungs. Finally—too much to bear—he blanked out from pain. Soon after he died, the nurse looked me in the eye, instructed, "We say he died peacefully." Air is blowing, tide is rising, and the gulls are screeching.

When I read Brother Adam's obituary in the *New York Times*, I was captivated. I xeroxed the image of his face on a piece of onionskin paper and tacked it above my desk. As I was writing about the death of a close friend, her death transformed into his. I never met Brother Adam.

THIS IS MY BROTHER TALKING

The little I knew about it was a source of terror. Of fear and terror. Of being terrorized by the *thought* of having polio.

I remember a spinal tap of some kind being done to you, uh, some tests being done. I have a hard time remembering details of, say, beyond a point of, actually I was pretty old—there's a block, a mental block that set in at some point. But in terms of just . . . I remember a doctor coming and tests being done in your, in the house. I remember that it was extremely painful. It was described that way, and the whole thing was petrifying. *Petrifying.*

I don't remember if anyone said *polio* in our house that day, but it was clearly more serious than *anything* that had ever happened. Nothing came close. You know, whatever incidents, illness, it was on a level of concern that was different.

And it's . . . the next thing I remember is you being taken away in an ambulance. I have a very vivid memory of that.

You remember the house? You came up the stairs, and it was sort of half levels coming up, turning corners. After the first level there was a little room over the garage, and I remember looking out the window, holding Maggi in my arms, and seeing the ambulance pull away.

This is a separate incident, walking on Pryor Lane, or maybe biking. Somebody's brother had had polio, maybe Tyner Corning's brother or Roy Halstead, or maybe it was John Barmack. Anyway, it was a friend, and his brother had had polio a year or two earlier. And, uh, I think I was the one who said it. *"Let's get off this street. Let's go in a different way."* It was like, you know, it was a plague.

This was before you got sick—it wasn't in our family yet—but that's how I saw it. If someone had it, you would go in the opposite direction. Turn around and go as far away from it as you could.

You getting polio was a crisis that changed the life of our family. Being right in the cauldron of polio was a whole different thing than even a neighbor having it. Instead of being afraid of this mysterious thing, the mysterious thing all of a sudden, was . . . was in my house. The *thing* being the disease. And so it wasn't a mystery anymore. It went from being a total mystery to being inside the walls of the house where I lived.

The day you got it, I had just finished my paper route. You were helping me. We were on our bikes. I took the paper route very seriously, and I timed it every day. I knew how long it would take and tried to do it as quickly as I could. I'd prepare the papers, put little rubber bands on them, so I could dispatch each paper a little bit faster. I got it down to under twenty minutes.

Then I remember holding a little baby—Maggi was an infant—in the window. The picture of standing in the window is a *marker*, it's a *time marker*. Maggi was helpless, and I was too. Just as helpless.

Those letters I sent you in the hospital—I sure had a way of not saying anything. I didn't know what to say. I just told you whatever. I just threw words on a page that had nothing to do with anything. I just filled the obligation to send a letter. Just reading them now, there's no substance, no merit at all.

I mean, I didn't know what to say. Like a diary of meaningless things! "I got a basketball uniform." It gave you a letter to open, took five seconds of your time to read. What you got was something from me that was absolutely forgettable, 100 percent.

I remember not being able to get into the hospital. I have a clear picture of being outdoors and trying to see you from a window, and I don't—and I didn't see you. I couldn't go in because of my age and I tried to get to a window. I might have gotten a glance . . .

The wheelchair wasn't nearly as devastating as the cast. The cast was—I mean, you saw people in wheelchairs, like if a person broke their leg or something, but the cast was not believable.

I sort of remember being told that you were coming home, and you had a cast on, and it was not a small one. And in fact it ran from your forehead to your waist, or maybe even a little below—I don't remember exactly—and it would eventually be reduced in size, but when I saw it, it was a *shock*. It was a shock to see the massive size of the cast and that you were, the fact that you were . . . it was shocking to see. You were a *prisoner*. At that time, the thing I got the greatest pleasure from was being able to run out of the house and jump over a fence and do a somersault. Physical activity meant everything to me! And . . . and basically you were unable to have any physical activity whatsoever. You had to be rolled over. You had to have a bedpan. That was a devastating thing to see. In the house.

If I was ashamed, maybe I blocked it out. I know I had friends come over and see you and some sort of normal contact did materialize. I don't know how long it took. My guess is the idea of having a friend come to see you, at first, was unthinkable. Yeah. It was something beyond belief.

I remember the bed. It was a hospital bed in the far right corner of the television room that got cranked up and cranked down. And you had a tutor, Mr. Markowitz. I remember 'cause I liked him a lot.

You know, I guess the change of being afraid of the unknown of this disease and then having it be your own sister and in your own home, hey! It became a reality very quickly! It was the basics of just functioning. That's what the focus was. In terms of just, *Okay, life goes on.* Friends are going to come here as they did before. And . . . it was adapted to.

When I got used to you being sick, once you were living at home for a year, two years, I decided that I was *never* going to fight with you again, and basically anything you wanted to do was just fine with me.

HOSPITAL SNAPSHOTS

Vashti's about to give me a sponge bath, but I'm saying "Vashti, please, take one of me."

Yesterday my father gave me a camera. My arms can move, and my right hand is fine, I think. Vashti's skin is shiny and black. Her uniform is starched white. I just took a picture of her. She's laughing her deep roll of a laugh. "Okay," she says. I'm naked, but there's so much heat on this ward that I'm not cold. The electric outlet right by my bed sometimes shoots fire out at night. When I try to turn my head to see, it's gone.

Vashti turns me on my side. I lie there, my arms covering my yet-to-develop breasts. *Click*.

My doctor is on the ward. I hear his voice down the hall. Vashti starts the sponge bath. Vashti Thompson, I love her.

It's night. it's winter. Steam in the air is clouding the window next to my bed. I keep waking up. Crows near the glass swoop close and caw. I love my Brownie Hawkeye.

There I am in a wheelchair! There I am on a stretcher being lowered into a whirlpool bath! There I am lying flat in the hospital bed stark naked, laughing, looking directly into the camera! Listen to what my brother wrote, he's so great.

> I saw those pictures. I sure wish I could swim in that swimming pool and that last picture whew!! Would you like a few pinup calendars. Ha Ha.
>
> Love,
> Richard Esquire (and I don't mean the calendar) Block

INSIDE THE WHIRLPOOL

When the nurse comes down the hall with her clicking-her-shoes walk, it's about to start. She rolls me onto a canvas stretcher, wheels me to the whirlpool room where the world is closed on top. A mechanical pulley lifts the stretcher across the whirling water and lowers me slowly with a grating sound. Down I go under the flushing water. My ears hurt. Sometimes the nurse's hands feel nice.

"Playland," I say when Patsy asks, "If you could be anywhere, where would you be?" I love the roller coaster. All you do is scream. Now look at me. Lots of metal and gizmos and machines. Smelly steam. It stinks.

Like a baby in a crib, I concentrate on my feet, gaze at my toes and knees. My limbs, my legs, their shape particularly mine. Me and not me and the line between. What is the boundary between everything else and my body?

In the whirlpool, I notice that my breasts are beginning to develop—it's sexy to see. When I am clothed and older, I will dive from a rowboat, flirt with a man so he will never get over seeing the clothed and wet me. But here—no lake, no trees. The nurse takes a picture of me.

Whirling bubbles jostle my leg. Passive, from above, my eyes watch. I have forgotten what it's like to want to run and to run at the same time. To think and do with no interruption in between. No chasm.

In the whirlpool, how far away my feet look. Two feet, two legs. One leg, another leg. Starting from my chest, I look all the way down my body, down into the water. My floating legs waver around. All my toes, each separate. Floating legs, floating toes, floating feet, far from me. Now for my fingers. I focus.

A floating arm, a hand, closer to my brain, my home now.

Flex your fingers, I tell myself. One moves, then the other. There.

"Come, dear, do your other hand now," says the nurse. I look at floating fingers. Water moves my hand, young and plump but thinning from lack of use. Water on my bedsores, smoothing and soothing.

As the nurse tells me to keep exercising, I see my vagina halfway down from head to toe, a mile away. No hair there yet. I focus on it, slow down my mind, block out the nurse's voice, stop my exercise.

Bubbles there, on my vagina. I'm in a jungle-like aviary. Birds fly to the top of the closed dome, teetering, twittering, longingly looking up at the sky through the curving glass. They butt their heads on the dome to escape.

I'm in this jungle pool, seething black, perfectly round, a princess thrown in, sacrificed. People toss in rubies, gold. Ruins—there are too many in this hospital ward. That girl with breaking bones that don't grow, that boy with sticklike legs who will never walk, Jeff in braces, his legs heavier than lead, like a robot's.

I need to strengthen my neck. The whirlpool motor turns off. It's quiet now.

WALKING

Prisoners outside walk by my Sunshine Cottage windows. A cloud of men in grey uniforms, the sky grey too. More grey on the ward walls, all things the same. On their own, my lungs are working.

I'm in bed and can't get up. My legs are flesh-toned sticks, starting from my buttocks. Sometimes I feel blood run through them. My knees are freezing.

There's a girl whose legs are chopped off above the knee—why is *she* here? She purposely leapt in front of a subway, they say.

I can't do anything myself. When I want *anything*, I have to ask for help. This I hate the most.

It's so hard to stand up. The main thing is to get upright and lean against the bed. My tight hand grips the metal side of the bed. I've got to stand. I smile at Dad taking a picture of me.

"Praise the lord with your feet," a nurse said, and I think she's right. I think my feet are unusually great.

My father takes pictures of me in the wheelchair. They have a certain cachet, a glamour I have never had before or since. My large eyes are fixed on faraway places. But in the photos, my head nods down as if my neck has no muscles, like a newborn's.

I look hard at my legs to send them strength. I walk between the parallel bars. I am weak like a weed just pulled from the garden, lying on the ground.

MUD

In a blur, my husband has left. I am walking in the snow where I used to live, in a wind. All I want is to sleep, shut my eyes, not say a thing. I throw off my clothes, turn to the wall. My flesh has forgotten itself. I am gone.

"Follow me," says the man who will become my second husband. We walk through a white-tiled corridor to an indoor pool in a room facing the sea. Later, out in the stinging air, we sing, strolling down the beach, "Cockles and mussels, alive, alive—o."

Back in our room, my eyes stop on his arms, his stocky torso. Every object shivers and charms. As he bends to turn out the lamp, I see his red underwear inch past the waist of his pants. I love the hair on his legs. "Come to bed," he says. He's never seen the inside of my house, but he's in my bed now, his tongue's in my mouth.

My hands veined, not young and plump, we drive through Napa Valley like babies—drink wine, take mud baths.

An attendant at the mud bath motel is dressed in white. She lays me down on a piece of body-sized plywood. She slides me off the board into the tub of volcanic ash mud. In the steam, my legs stretch far, my body one thing, my head another.

I used to hate steam rooms and indoor pools, their putrid stink reminded me of sick. The wet feel on the bottom of your feet as you walk on the tiles. Staleness creeps up through you, contaminates, starts with your feet.

At a resort with my older son, he sweats in the steam room, then leaps into the pool. Copying him, to the steam room I go, drop the sheet on the floor, stretch across the wooden slats, sweat. I rise up, dash to the cold hotel pool, and dive with no reserve.

Coming out of the water, I look at my son's beautiful face, the little mark above his lip. I remember that day when he was two and fell face first onto a metal doormat and cut his lip. The moment returns—the blood, the moment my boy is threatened.

Rosy pink adobe, ochre, cocoa brown, years later. In a hot tub in the out of doors, cold wind on my cheeks, my body soaks. Milky green growth blankets these spacious acres. Frost melts off the plastic cover. Yesterday I used a rubber mallet while laying a brick floor with my younger son; my grandson is about to be born.

My son loves birds, used to lie on the ground as a little boy, sunflower seeds sprinkled around him. Chickadees would feed right next to him.

Floating outside, I look up. A jet streams across the sky. Two white lines blur, merge. A plane crosses. Sound all over—pitches, tones—loud and soft. Traffic on a nearby highway. I hear birds. A dog barks.

Through the woods, a makeshift bridge crosses the arroyo. A clock painted on a tree keeps time that never moves. I'm flexing my feet, keeping time with the highway buzz and hum. Shadows of aspen on the chocolate wall.

Suddenly the shadows look upside down. I curl in the hot tub, can't breathe from the steam—got to get out. Laying the brick floor with a rubber mallet, but there was another rubber mallet.

The doctor helps me sit—I can picture it in a blur. I'm wearing pink shortie pjs. He takes out a rubber mallet, taps my knee, which does not move a bit. I am very sick.

GRANDMA CELIA MAIL

Dear Karen,

This get well card is from your dear Grandma Celia's brother Maurice, who together with my whole family wish you a speedy recovery. Darling, we have not seen you in a long time, but we remember your sweet face. Please for everyone's sake and especially for your Grandma Celia's sake who loves you more than anyone else in the world, hurry and get well.

Dear Darling Karen—I do not know what to write you, except that I want you to get well real soon. I would like to see you if possible.

I would like to buy something for you, but I do not know what you would like.

So long my sweet Karen and try to get well real soon,

Your Grandma Celia that loves you very much

My Sweet Beautiful Granddaughter—I would love to see you. I am thinking of you day and night.

I am making a pretty pleated skirt for you. I wish to know what you would like to have. I would buy you anything.

I will try to see you if they will let me in. So long Darling Karen

Love and Kisses
Your Grandma who loves you Very Much

My Sweet Beautiful Karen—I wish I could see you, but it seems there is no chance.

I was in your house. The snapshots of you look beautiful. Your mommy and daddy told me that you are feeling much better. I hope it will not be very much longer, and you will be home.

I wish you could write to me just a few words, it would make me very happy. My darling Karen I think of you all the time.

Your Grandma Celia
Who loves you very much

Dear Celia,

I hope by this time you have snapped out of that terrible shock of Karen's condition. Believe me it struck all of us like a bombshell. My heart goes out to that child. I hope and wish the case is mild. Yes this is life Celia and we have to take everything in stride. If what we all wish for, for that child will materialize—I hope she'll be ok . . .

Your brother,
Maurice

TAKE THINGS IN STRIDE

Polio weakened one side of my body more than the other. Eventually, as I exercised, the stronger side got stronger faster than the weaker, so I became hunched over. Two years after I got sick, an operation to correct this curvature stopped my growth.

The doctors had wanted to wait until I reached full height, but there was danger in the wait. I was curving with such speed that they thought my heart might get squeezed. Then my heart would stop. I was supposed to have been taller than five feet.

To straighten my spine, I was put in a body cast that went up my neck and down one leg to the knee, stopping above my hip on the other side. A pie-shaped chunk was cut from the middle, a turnbuckle attached to it. Everyday the doctor came and tightened the turnbuckle. Finally, when my back was straight, I had the spinal fusion.

The doctors cut a window in the back of the cast and then cut a groove through thirteen vertebrae. They implanted a long bone from a bone bank—whose was it?—closed me up, replastered the window shut, and for a year I stayed in bed while my bones fused with this stranger's spine.

When I first arrived at the hospital, they took me to a room for four people. Two were in plaster casts that went over their heads and down one leg to the knee. A hole for the face was cut from the plaster. A third girl was screaming that she would not have her hair cut.

My brown hair went halfway down my back. The hospital barber came to my room. Before I knew it, he gave me a crew cut. Then I was taken to a large room with windows all across one wall, looking out to the East River.

The day was extraordinarily sunny. There was a metal rack in the room. My arms were tied to two bars and my legs to two others. I was thirteen, with a crew cut and hunchback, spread-eagled on a metal rack. It felt sexual. Doctors wrapped rolls of hot wet plaster around me until I was caged in a huge shell, immobilized. As the plaster dried and hardened, it burned like fire.

The flash of the flashbulb bursts across the black glass. In the photo, I'm looking at my father in a handheld mirror as he takes the picture. My bed's in front of the window, a crooked venetian blind half up, me in a massive cast, metal all around—bed, bars, side table, venetian blinds. Glass and plaster, everything hard. The only soft thing in the photo is me—my framed face, my hands, my arms.

When my brother's friends visit, one of them picks up a scissors and knocks on my back, metal on plaster. We all break out laughing at the loud *clunk*.

Windsor by Revlon, Red Tinge, Red Orange—which color to paint my nails? Me, the secret siren laid up in bed.

Feeling ALL WASHED UP?
It's a Dirty Shame!

The only word I like in this get-well card that just came is *dirty*, but I like what Patsy writes:

> Too bad you can't neck in the cast—isn't it? Can you live without booze for long? Well maybe I will bring you a little—what do you prefer Sherry or Gin? I think I know.
>
> I just finished a real disgusting book called "Marjorie Morningstar." It has some real dirty parts which you would enjoy I'm sure or have you reformed? I doubt that.

Patsy says things like *superjazzy, fab, terriff* and *damned straight,* words I like.

> "I am so glad the operation is over—it will not be long and you will have a figure—I bet like some model. With that beautiful sweater!!"

This note from our housekeeper, Gertrude, gave me the idea to write to the Barbizon School of Modeling as a joke. They just wrote back.

REPORT ON QUALIFICATIONS

We wish to acknowledge your interest in modeling but since you are not as yet of a suitable modeling age we would not be able to determine at this time if you have the physical qualifications for a career in modeling.

You are at an age when you are still growing and your facial appearance and figure measurements are and will be changing. For this reason it would be best that we see you when you are somewhat older.

The food here stinks—I smell the food cart a mile away. Sam the black orderly sneaks out and brings us back pizza pies.

I love one of my doctors, Dr. Hass. I love my brother's friend Gordo van Nes. I love Sam, and tell him so in a note.

Dearest Sam,

I have been madly in love with you for years. Every time I see you my heart gives an extra beat. I cannot express my love in a letter. So please don't forget to meet me by the bridge, near the river, in front of Hospital for Special Surgery. I will be wearing clothes.

Love Always,
Your Lover

I love Jerry. His room is down the hall. He is paralyzed, in a wheelchair. He's Irish, from the Bronx. Has lots of freckles and curly red hair. He can move a lot compared to me. We realized that if I was on a stretcher in the room with the TV and no nurses were around, he could wheel up to me and we could make out. We do it now, a lot.

I lay in bed encased in plaster, turning from a little girl into a teenager as doctors tried to make me normal. I wrote to the Barbizon Modeling School, I got my period, I was a butterfly in a cocoon.

BUSTIERS, BRACES, AND NOISE

My first spring at Sarah Lawrence College, it's like black nothing living in the dorm, being away from home. Like I'm floating and can't reach the ground. Like I'm driving fast, I feel the road, the car is making contact, but not enough. We're reading Camus' *La Peste*.

I like taking the train into New York City and walking down to that French bookstore for paperbacks, the pages uncut, the paper off-white and rough.

Green glass raffia-covered Chianti bottles decorate my dorm room. I'm reading James Baldwin. With a scratchy Edith Piaf record on, drinking green Pernod, I fall asleep, dream of bustiers. A tall man, voted most handsome, hands me a pink rubber bustier and says, "You have to wear it." I can't. I don't know how. I want to, but I think it won't look good, so I say, "I just can't." He says, "You have to." All I want is to be home. Be there. Stay there. The bustier is not exactly pink, I come to realize. It is tan. And it is not exactly a bustier. It is a back brace. I shove it in some attic.

When I go to the city I do not shop. I'd rather just walk. In department store dressing rooms, those mirrors reflect so you see yourself from behind. Seeing my back dismays me because I tend to forget that a scar runs the length of my spine. I could walk forever and never be bored. I walk all the way down to Washington Square Park.

It's sunny, early spring, and cool. My reddish brown hair is pulled back in a long ponytail. There are pearl earrings in my newly pierced ears. The sweater I wear is Norwegian, the buttons grey metal the size of my thumbnail, with crocheted blue loops for buttonholes. I'm wearing a pleated skirt that day, no idea what shoes.

I sit on the rim of the fountain, reading. A man who might be thirty sits beside me and begins to chat. His hair is combed back, looks wet, like he's come straight from the shower. He sees my books, asks what I think of Camus, says he's a writer. There's distance between us as we sit on the concrete rim of the fountain. The sun is getting hotter.

He asks me back to his apartment on Perry Street. When I get there, I go to pee, notice a peach chenille robe hanging on the bathroom door. My head is like concrete, fixed, nothing inside moving. But seeing that chenille bathrobe cracks it a little.

His living room is small. A window behind the sofa looks down a shaftway of grey light. I sit down on the couch and start to talk.

He's lunging at me. This can't be. He's picking me up and carrying me to his bed. Tediously he undoes my sweater as I punch and squirm. My arms are swinging, I can see, but my sweater is off. He pushes up my skirt, takes his long penis out, and tries to put it in me.

I see my legs kicking, my shoes on. I switch from swinging to noise. I yell so loud that his body begins to shrink back. I shoot up, grab my sweater, and run outside.

That noise, it was worth the world.

My husband, our two young sons, and I lived in one of those large West Side of New York apartments with a maid's room off the kitchen. A huge wooden table scavenged from a boarded-up fish store was my worktable in the maid's room, where I made mirror collages for years.

I'd load my sons into a stroller and walk down Columbus Avenue to the trash heap at the glass and mirror store. I'd rigged a strong bag to the stroller handle to hold discarded mirror scraps. We'd walk home, the boys would go off to play in their room, and I'd go to my worktable. It was a good time.

There is a way to shatter mirrors so you don't get cut. Put one in a heavy plastic bag, flat on the table, and hit it with a hammer. Hold the hammer a foot from the surface and control its fall. All the slivers are contained in the bag. Slowly, gingerly, pull them from the bag.

To make a mirror collage, use a piece of wood as your canvas. Play with the shattered scraps on the wood until the images you see (sometimes of yourself) excite you. Pile the slivers, move them around. When you're ready, glue them down. Your reflection shifts!

TRY THIS

Like a wide field of uneven rows, stretch marks from having borne my large sons cover my asymmetrical belly. These wavy rows of shiny skin have been here since I became a mother at twenty-one.

I have a packet of nude photos that my husband took of me, my back especially. "It's the way I'll really be able to see what my scar looks like," I told him. This is Paul, my second husband. After I got divorced, I wanted to find a man who loved me for my body, and I did.

I was too bold and curious for my own good. The sight of my back is too much, so I toss the packet into the garbage pail. Later, as I grab a glass of water, I glance at the garbage. *These photos must be destroyed.* I open the envelope, squeeze in a lime, God knows why. After dinner, I scrape our plates into the envelope, scallion bits, leftover veal loaf.

Why didn't I just cut the damn things up? No way can I sleep. Two a.m. turns to three. What, I start to wonder, is happening to them? Maybe the lime juice is causing a chemical change? Finally I sleep. Alchemy.

It's morning, I'm drinking coffee, digging down to the bottom of the garbage, rescuing the slimy packet. I toss it in the sink, crack an egg into it. This is becoming a scientific experiment. As I squish the envelope, mush the contents, my husband takes a bite of bagel, doesn't see what I'm up to. He leaves for work.

Inside the envelope, it's eggy, gooshy, very yellow. I separate the pictures under running water.

The surface has given way! With my fingernails, I scratch the softness. Bright yellow lines appear. Inspired, I fill a plastic bowl with clear, cold water, drop each photo in to keep it workably wet, clear a space on my desk. By day's end, my yellow lines embellish the photos, each one now transformed into *something else*.

By the time they dry, they have little to do with my body. I take them to Staples to have them enlarged and copied. John, a uniformed man in a red shirt and black pants, waits on me. People are busy copying pages, posters, signs. We experiment with the machine, dark settings, light settings, in between. Some take color away, some add it. Tone the yellow down, no, intensify it, leave the pink, keep the flesh fleshy. We never mention the subject.

After a long while, an overweight blond clerk comes to relieve John. In her red shirt and black pants, she stands over the laser copier. John shows her how to work the images. I'm fussing at the counter with stapler, White-Out, scissors. I do not want these images in anyone but John's hands, but he needs a break.

She steps back from the copier, comes toward me. "I saw what was behind the scratches and I *had* to walk away." She swallows, sighs, she gulps, looks straight at me.

"Do you get paid for this? Do you display these?"

"They have to do with a book I'm writing," I say.

She paces to the cash register, waits on a customer. Her breathing is labored. She returns to me.

"Is it a romance novel? Is there a murder in it?"

"It's a kind of memoir."

"A what?"

To write a memoir or anything at all, you want a little inspiration. I love what Jean Cocteau said: "Inspiration is the result of a profound indolence and of our incapacity to put to work certain forces in ourselves."

Try this. Go to a thrift shop. Buy a bolster with back and sides. If it's ripped in the back, all the better. Collapse onto the bolster. Make a roost. Write a sentence or two.

Or try this. Order a ton of Chinese takeout. Eat it all. You're so heavy when you get in bed that it's hard to move. Maneuver your body to turn over. Then, on your stomach, hoist yourself up by your elbows, as if you have no lower body muscle. Then move to your desk and start to write.

Or rent a couchette on an overnight train to Georgia. Lock your cubby, set up the bed, get undressed. Put the light out, open the shade, look out. Masturbate through the whole state of Virginia in the dark.

You won't sleep much. Cover on, cover off. When it's on, too heavy. When it's off, you float too free. Quilt too hot, too heavy. Sheet too light, too cold. Listen to the sound of night. Wait. As you slide deep down in the bed, make up sentences for what seems like forever until morning's first light.

CLOTHES AND HAIR

"They sewed her up with silk just like a little roast pig." The night nurse doesn't know I'm listening because I'm still sick from the operation, my eyes glued shut. She wears nail polish a shade of red like blood. She's fat and square like a block. A large needle in my arm, I can't move. Her voice is loud.

Dreaming of war, marching through the Russian steppes single file, shoeless through the snow. I scrounge for clothes to cover my crooked body, one shoulder higher than the other.

My Russian grandmother sewed clothes in a sweatshop in New York on the Lower East Side. Going backwards in time, clothes and history intersect. The early fabric of last century when immigrant women hunched over sewing machines, saving money so their sons could go to school in this gold and green land. Grandma Celia worked for the fashion designer Adele Simpson, sewed a brown shirred dress for my mother.

In Grandma Celia's presence, my parents made fun of her narrow-minded worldview, kicked each other under the dining room table. She dropped straight pins all over the floor since she was careless and sewed all the time. She sewed me a coral coat and leggings with a white bunny rabbit collar, told me how fast I used to run—even in her nineties, about to die. "I dreamt I was cooking you a chicken!" she burst out that final day as I walked into her room. That's what she said when she was dying.

Her hair went to her waist. She wore it braided in a bun on top of her head. My hair's always been long too. I love how it trails behind me in the water when I swim fast. When I come out of the water, I love how it slooshes down my back.

Today I am in the hospital about to get a crew cut. Did I tell you why? Because I'm going into a full-length body cast that goes around your head, with a little window so your face can look out. That's why you have to get your hair cut off.

Suzy Last, my best friend here, is getting a crew cut too. Her hair is like the flank of a horse—black, heavy, sleek. It's strong and goes where it wants. Mine is fine and thin and does whatever you want. If you think "Curl into a pageboy," kazaam, it will. I used to wear mine in braids or two bunches. Now I love it loose. When I was little, my mother tried to comb it neat. She'd part it three ways, make a ponytail on top. Hair fell free on the sides and back. My hair gets chestnut from the sun. The strands are soft.

A few other girls are getting casts too. Irene is already in hers. The windows in the room are huge, but the light today is so dull that the city seems covered in plastic sheets.

"Baldy," I call to Irene across the room. She shoots me a look. "Why do you have to call me that? I don't like it."

The barber is here to cut Angela's hair. She keeps yelling, "No!"

"I come back tomorrow," Tony says. Angela's hair goes down to her butt.

"You can't, I won't! I'm not having it cut!"

Angela went home. No crew cut. No surgery. When I told my mother, she shook her head. "Angela's vain," she said.

Once I was in the cast, we found huge cotton men's pajamas to fit over it, in little blue and white checks, with a drawstring tied to keep the bottoms on. But it was not cloth that touched my skin but plaster, weighty, white, hard.

I'm in college and in New York City for the weekend. It's raining, and the photographer's window faces tree branches covered with droplets turning to ice. He is rubbing my pubic area. My body is a map. I wear a lot of black clothes, bohemian style, and have a long ponytail, and came to the city for fun. He just pushed my beige silk slip up past my hips, the back of it cut low so my scar shows.

He gets up from the bed and goes to a cupboard, meticulously opens a pack of Pall Malls. I lie there, absorbed by tree limbs lit by the rosy streetlight. He smokes quietly. My body feels lively.

A faded pink and green cloth is tacked to the sloped ceiling. I arch my buttocks slightly. He walks down the hall, opens a cupboard, small sounds of rummaging. He hesitates. Does he have a girlfriend? Cabinet closes, water runs.

As a teen, I once sat on the edge of a swimming pool wearing a low-backed bathing suit, and a man my father's age sat beside me and said, "You have a beautiful back." Then again, another man said, "I've never slept with anyone deformed before." The photographer's sheets feel good. As it begins to get dark, he positions me in my slip, on my side. Early evening low light. He has been taking pictures of me since we met, in my slip or my full white skirt with nothing on top. He shows and hides my scar at once. He does not mention my scar, nor do I.

He slowly walks down the long corridor back to his bedroom, where I have not moved. He has baby oil. A draft comes in from a window crack. From a closet, he removes a red plaid robe, which he drapes over my back.

The telephone rings. He sits on the bed, he is touching my back. Finally he picks up.

He hangs up the phone, removes the robe, pulls the sheets off, sets his tripod up. From the Con Ed Plant down the street, neon smoke rises.

THE SWAMP

It's that summer before I got sick. Patsy and I are rambling around on our bikes on dirt roads, exploring the swamps near the Sound. We stop where the steps go down to the water, lean our bikes against a tree. It's hot. It's a bad summer for polio. We don't care.

As we sit on the warm stone steps, Patsy tells me she made the swim team. The surface of the water, I notice, is blackish and flat. Something is moving right underneath. Patsy is talking. Her voice is starting to sound far away. For a second, I think of winter, how the Sound almost freezes sometimes. Now it's like the top of the water is whispering.

"An eel! Patsy, an eel!" It's long and black. It's riding underneath the water. I careen up the steps, jump on my bike, peel out toward home. At dinner, my father explains that people eat eels, which sounds bad to me.

When my father and I go crabbing, he rows, and I sit on the back seat and watch. I like the hair on his freckly, sunburned arms. We have a string net on a long wood pole, and he rows up close to the rocks at the edge of the inlet. I keep my eyes fixed on the water. When I see a crab on a stone, I sneak the net in, swoop it up fast.

I balance on the post-and-rail fence as Mrs. Baker snaps my picture out back by the crabapple tree. I'm wearing a see-through blue pastel dress. My thin arms are pink and strong. I'm smiling like I'm supposed to. My brother's at school, and my baby sister is I don't know where. Today the photographer is taking me.

As she says, "Why don't we try some profiles, dear," she twists my head toward the Sound like it's the screw top of a jar, points my chin up, rearranges my arms and legs, repositions my torso, trying to make me look a certain way, which I let her do. Which is a big deal, considering I'm a squirmer.

"Now, dear, please look right straight up into that big blue sky." Which is exactly what I'm doing because there's a low-flying little plane making a lot of noise. "Mrs. Baker, Mrs. Baker!" I screech. "Something's wrong with the plane! Mom! Mom! Where's Mom?"

My body goes limp. The plane swoops lower and lower.

It's near the trees. The plane is falling into the trees. First I can't move, then my body fills with liquid, and I dash from the fence, dash off into the overgrown brush of the back lot, my dress catching on pricker bushes, my arms getting scratched. I reach a piece of smoking fuselage. A policeman is already there. "Started to go down near the junior high, steered it off toward the water, then he parachuted. Lucky no one got hurt." Sirens, fire engines—I have got to get home.

A different day, near dinnertime, Patsy and I start toward home on our bikes. It's August. Four boys, the ones from Catholic school who live up on Lion's Hill, bike toward us. "Hey, wanna play bicycle tag?" one yells. "Sure," we say. All six of us come to a stop, straddle our bikes in the middle of the road. One boy yells, "You're it!" They crash onto their bikes, turn around, race back toward the swamp. We pedal, we fly. They sweep around the big curve, disappear onto the dirt road near the Sound where we often explore. They slow down, bump along. At last we tag them.

They've stopped. They're standing by their bikes, looking at us, each one waiting for the others to speak. Patsy and I get off ours. They walk toward us. One grabs my wrist. Another grabs Patsy. One of them takes out a knife: "Go ahead, dirty Jews, follow Billy."

There's a narrow path stamped down through the high swamp grass. They've planned this. We're being led deep into the brush. When we get to a clearing, they tie our hands. Sobbing, I keep repeating, "Please let us go." They mumble to each other, seem to disagree. I start yelling at the top of my lungs.

"Okay," one says, "get outta here fast! We never want to see you on Lion's Hill, ya hear?" One of them rips up a piece of swamp grass by its roots. "See this? That kid who got polio, he got it from playing in the swamp grass over by Pryor Lane. Get out of here or we'll rub it all over you. You'll turn into little cripples."

Now it's fall. The bell rings—time to start walking home from school for lunch. I feel a little sick. It's Book Week, and my book report is due tomorrow. I hope my mother makes pb and j today.

I barrel down the school stairs, glance up at the ceiling, which looks hollow like the blue sky. Whoops, almost tripped running down the stairs. I don't feel like giving the book report. Wish I could stay home tomorrow.

There—there's a good stone to kick. I always find one to kick home. The next day, I'm in an ambulance, speeding to the hospital.

THIS IS PATSY TALKING

The day you got sick was like nothing else that ever had happened. I mean, in life. Certainly it's the outstanding event of childhood, unlike anything else. Because at that age, you know, you don't think about life and death and then it's in your face!

I don't know that I knew what life and death meant, but I remember my father asking your father if it was okay to pray for you. And your father said that even though he wasn't a believer, he wasn't sure it wouldn't help, and we should go ahead and pray.

My father took us into the den facing East, with his yarmulke and his shawl, the tallis, and wrapped it around us, and we prayed.

The ambulance came. And I remember rushing over to your house. Not knowing what was going on. They're such buried memories.

We had to go and get some kind of shot they thought would help if you were exposed to polio. Gamma globulin, yes. The dosage varied based on your weight. I was upset because I was overweight, had to have this big dosage. Yes, rushing to a doctor. My sister and I calling people to say they better do this.

Then one day my mother took us to the hospital, and Richard and your mother came. They were allowed to go in your room, and we were told we couldn't because we weren't family. But we felt like family.

So we stood outside the window. I can still picture this big plate glass window—trying to talk to you, waving at you through this glass window, and it being so shocking to see you in there, but gratifying because it was right after we didn't know whether you were going to live or not.

And . . . remember how inseparable we were? We used to call each other when we were going out with our parents because the other person might call and wonder where we were. We used to laugh about it, call to say we were going to the bathroom.

When you went to the hospital, not only were you sick and the worry connected with that, but you weren't there to be my constant companion. You had some nerve! So I was kind of lost without having a best friend.

When you got sick it was a loss. It wasn't such a big loss in terms of—we didn't know at the beginning how long you'd be in the—how long were you in the hospital?

KAREN: A little over three months when I first got sick. That was the first time.

PATSY: Right. So it turned out *not* to be a really long time. It was the kind of time that seemed much longer because you were very sick. Nobody knew how you'd be. But once you were declared a survivor, and came home, I came to your house every day after school.

It was terrifying to see you in that horrible cast. That you'd never be whole again. And never be able to go back to running around. I didn't know if you'd be in a wheelchair afterwards or how crippled you would be. Nobody knew.

KAREN: Do you remember coming over to visit, and I'd be lying in bed barely able to move, and you'd come in, in this blue net gown to go to dancing class. What was that like for you?

PATSY (sighs): I don't remember that, but I'm sure it happened. I don't know, I think it was like you were a part of me. There was this part of me that was lying in the bed . . .

We didn't know that you'd ever be able to function. When you got out of that cast and were okay, it seemed such a miracle.

Sometimes I would try to imagine what it was like to be in that cast. I remember the stages. When it started there was a headband, and it was head to knee on one side and maybe thigh on the other, and then it got abbreviated to go across your chest, and that was a big day when you could take off that headpiece and have more mobility. Then it became a cast you could take off to take a bath. I remember your dying to take a bath and take that thing off. That was a big event to celebrate.

Do you remember the summer before you got sick, we read *Gone with the Wind*? I'd read a chapter, tear it out, and give it to you. I don't know which one of us was ahead.

I don't know why we didn't want to buy two books. It's a sort of strange thing to do, a strange way to read a book, but that's what we did. We shared one book, destroying it chapter by chapter.

Before you got sick, we used to steal—well, we didn't used to steal. There was this rough group up on Chatsworth Avenue, Margaret Somebody with bright red hair, a really attractive Irish Catholic girl. Anyway, there were these kids. We wanted to get into their group because they were fast. For us to get into their group, they said we had to steal something from the drugstore. It didn't matter what. It could be gum. And so we did. And we got caught and decided we didn't want to stay in the group because we couldn't keep up.

KAREN: I remember stealing, but not that we did it for a higher purpose. It was just fun. Remember the time we ran away?

PATSY: Yes! To that babysitter who lived across from school. We wanted to leave home because you were unhappy that Maggi was born. You were pissed that your parents weren't paying enough attention to you. So we ran to her house, and of course she called our parents. When my parents asked why I went along, I said, "Karen needed to get away."

KAREN: Do you remember that if I was at your house, and it got dark, and I had to walk home, I'd be scared. You'd stand at your door, and we'd keep yelling to each other until I got home?

PATSY: Yeah. That was before you got sick when there were no houses across the street and it was a huge woods. You know, after you got better, I think we thought polio was over.

SAYINGS

In my attic, I find what I call my polio pack, an old suitcase with photos, crucifixes, and mail that came when I was sick. There's an envelope with SAYINGS scrawled in turquoise ink across its front. In the hospital, for fun, I cut out scraps of words that struck me from movie magazines and *Hit Parade* and *Song Hits*. Then I glued them onto photographs I had taken with my Brownie Hawkeye:

Over six feet tall, muscularly built, with the brawn,
stamina and power of an all-American footballer

Was I thinking of FDR before he was struck or of a boy I liked?

Men Of Science

Was that for my father the food chemist, or for Jonas Salk?

All the girls are batty over Daddy-o

My father used to take me fishing in our rowboat. I found a photo of FDR alone in one. You can tell it's hot. He's pulled his trousers up so his thinned legs show under his braces. He's fishing. I've fished so much.

How history happens in photos, Jonas Salk in a white lab coat gazing down the camera's throat, or one of my father garbed in lab whites, staring through the lens.

I find a photo of me on a stretcher, taken about when Jonas Salk made the polio vaccine. In my Sayings envelope, I find a scrap—*National Relief*.

MR. DARK

The past has a funny name—Mr. Dark.

1954. It's spring, it's damp. I'm home from the hospital. The visiting nurse comes to have uncooperative me exercise. She has different-sized cans for me to grip as I lift my arms. I start with tomato paste, graduate to whole tomatoes.

I want a peanut butter and jelly sandwich. I have to call downstairs to ask my mother for it. I have to ask for everything.

If I ever walk again, I'll never forget this, I promise myself.

These words show me how fast I forgot. The present is the truest thing, the past is elusive, words fall short.

I'm an adult now. Days come around like white pages—lists, chores, bills, calls, lunch to fix, work to do, and on a good day, good sex.

I find myself in the basement. Half asleep, I've just had coffee. To spark memory, I pull out a pair of wooden crutches. I hobble about on the crutches, weave my way through the cellar mess, try to let my legs go limp.

It doesn't help. All I recall is the strength that grew in my arms. Then I think of how broad and strong FDR's arms became after he got sick.

Once I could finally walk, I went back to school in sixth grade for a year, wearing a back brace. The following fall I went into the body cast and had the back surgery. I hadn't been upright, vertical, for more than a year during that time. From my medical records:

9/5/56—This 13-year-old girl was re-admitted 11 months post-surgery. She had a spine fusion from D6 to L3. She now enters for new plaster, x-rays, and walking. She had poliomyelitis in 1953 involving her spine, right arm, back, abdomen and legs and left hand. Patient has been on tilt board this past week, progressive vertical tilting, so that she is now able to stand and walk. She is fitted in shoes and walks well.

In January 1957, I went back to school with no braces, no cast, a straight back, and zest. I skipped a grade, going into ninth grade instead of eighth. I did not look back. Right away, I had a boyfriend named Wesley, a handsome dark-haired fellow from the popular crowd. As the years went on, I barely mentioned my illness to a soul.

THE CAVE

I'm going to write about it. 1953. The year polio hit. In the room where I write, my cave, I'm settled down on my fluffy nest. I watch large snowflakes float past. The fire in the wood-burning stove is stoked up. I hope this blizzard never ends. Movement is curtailed, and that's what I love. On a mat on the floor, looking out the French doors, I'm nearly level with the blank white ground, sorry spring will come. This spacious haven, this hypnotic room where anything can happen.

If you get sick and then get better, you have to give your powerlessness up. That means you are once again the captain of your ship. But by then you have tasted sweet powerlessness, and it is not easy to forget.

Snow falling down. Flakes building up, walling me in, others out. White grows up the windows, inside sliced from out. Noiseless in this cell, my mind blank. I am trying to remember when I couldn't—and then could—walk.

Now the raspberry patch is vanishing under the white. The high, dark rhubarb stems just blew over and apart. Why does the bear in hibernation come out? I swear the sun is trying to.

I almost hear my mother saying, "Your Cream of Wheat is ready, steamy, a little lumpy, honey, your favorite!" I picture in the distance a long, polished old table with a white ironstone bowl on it. There's butter melting on the cereal and just the right amount of sugar. The table gets smaller as I try to walk to it.

Did you know that during World War II, Roosevelt would secretly return to his home in Hyde Park, New York, where he had a recurring dream. There he'd be, speeding down the hills on his sled in the deep snow.

I have a photo of him in the curing waters of Warm Springs, Georgia. Just his little face shows. Under water his legs are causing very small ripples. Water is holding him up.

The day before he got sick he had been fishing from a small boat, slipped overboard: "I'd never felt anything so cold. It seemed paralyzing, the icy shock." Then the forest fire he fought—Campobello, exhaustion, chills. Next day his thumb muscles got so weak he couldn't write. I too was photographed in water—same ripples across the photo. My face is gleaming, my hair, loose.

In my polio pack, there's a snapshot of me in braids. It's braidlike, how we all interweave.

In my Sayings envelope, I find

Don't Fence Me In
Yakety-Yak
The War Is Over

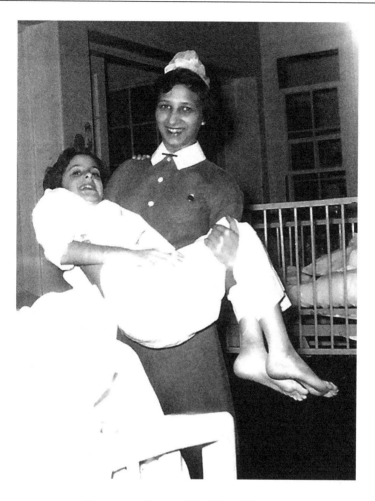

A nurse and me in Sunshine Cottage,
the polio ward at Grasslands Hospital in 1953

My best friend, Patsy Sternberg, looking at me
through the ward window

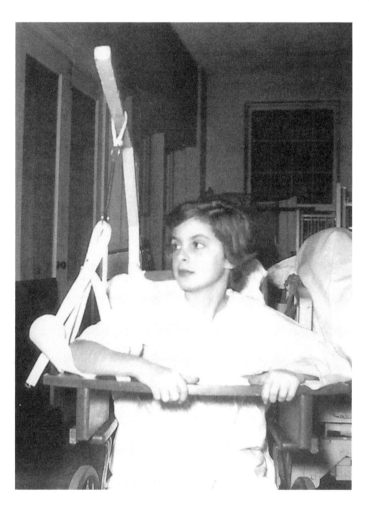

In the wheelchair

Vashti Thompson, my favorite nurse

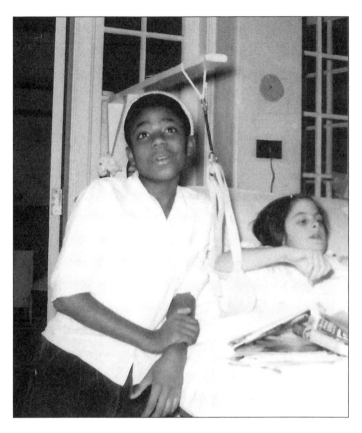

My friend Dennis, another patient on the ward, and me

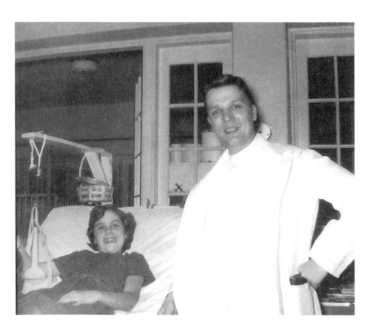

Dr. James Fishler, my doctor at Sunshine Cottage, and me

Dr. John Cobb, my doctor at the Hospital for
Special Surgery, in 1955

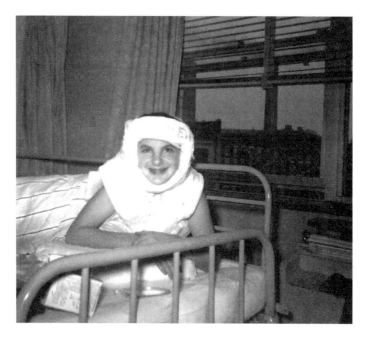

In the full-length body cast to correct my scoliosis

Sam, the nurse assistant, at the Hospital for Special Surgery

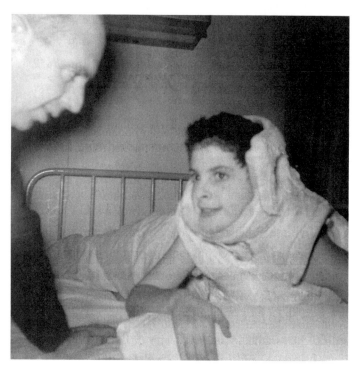

My father, Zenas Block, and me after part of the
plaster headpiece was removed

At home at 5 Flint Avenue in Larchmont, New York

My brother, Richard Block

My sister, Maggi Block, and me

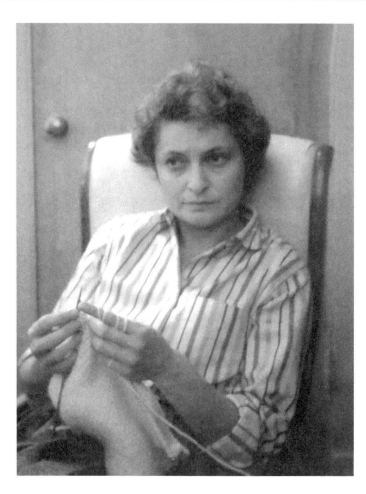

My mother, Lil Block

History looms small and large all at once.
Strike a match for history.

My sister, Maggi, campaigning for the March of Dimes

Plaque in front of FDR's homestead in Hyde Park, New York,
which I photographed in 1957